Time and Economic Intelligence of the 21st Century

A Divine Approach to Personal Strength and Success

By

Ijigban Daniel Oketa

Copyright

Copyright @ Ijigban Daniel Oketa and TFDC/HSPS. No part of this work must be reproduced or transposed without the prior written permission through the Author and publisher. (+234) 703-738-4814

ISBN-13:978-1537699837

Time and Economic Intelligence of the 21st Century- Ijigban Daniel Oketa

Table of Content

Introduction 4

There is no Hiding Place 12

Time Corrosiveness 17

The Spiritual Reformation and Restructuring 21

The Solution to Money 24

Time Deoxidization 31

There is a Partnership- HSPS 37

THE TWO LEGS OF HSPS 39

Understanding Your Power with God 45

Time Remains Evil Until Redeemed 47

The Natural VS the Supernatural 49

Apply an Action 54

Respect and Honour The Difference 56

Introduction

Money and time are synonymous as value system that can hardly be separated from each other. And a man's life is called time. Therefore how a man is able to manage his time is how he can successfully create his money.

A success mind set is not enough neither is a mere constant positive confession; we need to understand the way time works that influences our income and money and how to determine and manage our progress.

Money has a spiritual root and so is time. A man is a spirit and his spiritual understanding and subjection of money and time will really determine his success. Therefore time and economic intelligence is one's knowledge on how to order and to create time and money for a successful living. This is a higher spiritual order and must be put to practice for the best result in and out of life. The spiritual has a law of money and time. The application of one without the other may be productive but with minimal result. There is also a natural law or workings of money of money and time, but needs to be overrule by the supernatural for best results.

Where is the Money?

To the above question, many would say 'money is with the government, rich people, Church, banks etc' and they may be wrong. But to this question 'have you seen money today'? or 'do you have a piece of money at all?' The answer to the above may be yes and many persons may also add that 'but not enough for what I need" in all goodness and faith. Have you noticed that money seems not to be anywhere to be found? Even though many people talk about investment in business, in agriculture etc for and by the youth? The real challenge is that the needed money is not gotten or accessed. t may be surprising to inform you that even the federal, state and local government, the banks, churches and organizations are looking for the same money you are looking for.

What is Wrong

The government's bonds/equity are not selling. Bonds are just like a bank issuing Initial Public Offer (IPO) to raise investment capital but nobody seems to be interested even at it best rate. In another instance, the prices of the resources are low and its low state many countries are not buying. Now it is not a deliberate attempt no to buy but because it is not economically feasible for those countries as well. Some have chosen and developed other affordable or renewable forms of energy. And they are not also buying and finding alternatives because they are also experiencing the effect of the global economic depression in many areas like Nigeria. It means there are also in recession and facing the same problem (even worse) like your country. This is what is happening in the world and every nation is under the threat of complete downturn, system failures, money depletion or diminishing and social confusion.

The Laws of Money and Wealth

1. The first law of money and wealth states that everybody was once poor; but consciously some came out of poverty. Everyone was born into poverty irrespective of any background; if not why were you naked when you came on board?

2. That Money is not wealth until an investment is made in a life of a person. Consciously we can determine how

wealthy we go home; to live above poverty; and to improve the world.

3. Use the available money: More money was not created just because you and I were born into any country. Everyone is using the monies that are available. Find a way; a solution to allow money run to you.

4. A man's money and wealth is created and determined by himself not God. You must learn to create your money and wealth.

5. Creating Money and Wealth is a Partnership. Nobody actually owns any money; every money (value, goods etc) you have or hold is meant for exchange with a person or entity in order receive another per time.

6. The workings of money must be studied: this is to demonstrate your ability to sacrifice what you have for the knowledge (what) you need. Don't be

ashamed of money, wealth or prosperity or they will be ashamed of you. But just learn about them, obey their laws and they shall be yours.

PART ONE

Understanding the Global and National Recession and Social Crisis

Time and Economic Intelligence of the 21st Century- Ijigban Daniel Oketa

There is no Hiding Place

When a typical Nigerian admits that something is wrong and that they need help, then it has really got to the extreme. So, let us examine Nigeria as a case study here:

1. FGN says River Drys Up- Nature is fully at risk.
2. Inflation grew to over 17% officially
3. 351,000 lost their jobs in 8 months - 2016,
4. Oil prices dropped to $41 per barrel
5. GDP declines to a minus (-).
6. The price Fuel at N145/litre (after a 52% price increment) no longer sustainable – says NNPC.
7. We May Soon Stop Paying Civil Servants – CBN Alerts Nigerians
8. **Recession:** MTN Downsizes, Drops Davido, Banky W, Others as

Ambassadors - SIGNAL. Telecoms giant MTN have announced the 11 superstars that have been dropped

9. Zenith Banks Sacks over 1040 staff and also many other banks and organizations.

10. Someone sent this to me saying, *"I have being thinking why things are not working out well for my family. My heart is heavy. Has God forgotten us? Husband has come, but no money (to marry), I have a job but no salary. I cannot assist anybody not even my mother. Where have we gone wrong?"*

11. Another person posted on the social media saying *"In this (Nigerian) government of CHANGE, people can no longer pay their bills. States don't pay their workers anymore and those in federal agencies are under threat; terrorism gets worst and religious sentiments grow dangerously…."*

The list is endless. The above and many more is and how it is world-over. What God does now is to give us understanding of what to do to create our supply and supernatural blessing in what we need. And most times, He does so through someone; like Joseph, Daniel, Esther, Mordecai, King David and many others. Now it is your turn to turn things around for good where you are and worldwide. The greatest miracle is God using a man to provide solutions to others and to solve diversities of problems. From Europe to the Americas, the Caribbean, Austria, Asia and Africa, the cries of hopelessness and drought is heard without control. And we must respond individually through a global whole to order a proper restructuring. It doesn't matter the business you do, you are now in this business.

Our Inactions?

Our inactions and unbelief now will worsen the already existing confrontation to the extent that:

1. Rain will soon cease from the earth.

2. Diseases ten times worst than Ebola will come upon the world soon. It will make people sit at home for fear and not able work or feed.
3. Governments will be so poor that they may not be able to transit their leadership. General elections will be cancelled for lack of fund.
4. House animals (goats, cat, dogs, birds etc) will become very hostile to human beings even to their keepers and owners.
5. Lands will refuse to yield crops as they should and this will translate to higher degree of food scarcity.
6. Many economic systems and monetary policies will collapse totally. Depositor's moneys in commercial banks will disappear to tin air and many banks will fail.
7. Many government policies and employment schemes will fail at inception.

The Two Groups of People Worldwide

Two basic groups of people may emerge worldwide which include:-

1. **Those who will prosper exceedingly:** This set of people will be doing very little but will have many prosperous results. But they may become highly frustrated because of the burden of others round about them.

2. **Those who will suffer exceedingly:** This group will do everything to succeed but they will have very minimal results. They will certainly become highly discouraged. They will keep struggling to eat and to make ends meet daily. They will believe that government will help them or deliver the solution soon.

Time Corrosiveness

The current global crises is a spiritual mess and disorder called 'time corrosiveness' that has resulted in social, economic and political commotion in ruthless and diverse dimensions. Don't be in the dark. The world is not about to end and just believing in Christ or the confession of goodness will not solve the matter now. And if nothing is done in the right direction, this condition will linger and deteriorate for many years. And many people will take their own lives and even the lives of others for great anger and resentment. Every nation in the world will be affected evidently.

<u>Time Corrosiveness</u> is a system of gradual destruction of something by a more natural spiritual action; this, scientists may call chemical action. Now the solution has been found by a group and wish to teach people who need to succeed and how to use the solution for their own good. Once governments of nations are

aware, there will need those like you to educate citizens of their nations in order to recover their economies and contribute to global peace. Time corrosiveness affects value system; causes money diminishing and creates great uncertainties in livelihood and business.

The Global Nature with a Difference

Unlike other global economic recessions in time past, the current **global economic recession** is a forceful combination of **terrorism**, **corruption**, and **character deficiency**, **decline in societal value system** as well as **global warming**. Every economy and government is connected and interlinked with each other which make up the global economy or system. Therefore reason for the global nature is because the system of the world which includes many systems of money creation, value system and governments has failed. In a simple language, the world's leading spiritual system or believe has failed and becomes in effective. And now a new system is required to replace the old. Now we have found that system. Only those who obey the rules of <u>the new system</u> will survive the present age and create lasting peace and development across nations. This is why we need you to join hands to save the world, to save lives across cities and nations. It is possible and <u>we have begun already.</u>

Every problem has a solution; and this <u>global problem</u> at this time has a <u>global solution</u> which must be individually applied by us all. This is why we are here. The good news is that there is a solution now.

We care, and we have shared this with you.

PART TWO

Understanding the Solution

The Spiritual Reformation and Restructuring

All over the world, many clamor and protest for economic, social and political restructuring, and seem to be less concerned about spiritual restructuring. The question is, between spiritual restructuring and others (economic, social and political), which one comes first? If I heard you right, you said it is the spiritual and you are right. Therefore I challenge you that what is wrong with the world right now and your country has its solution rooted in the spiritual. Therefore what we need is a spiritual restructuring to order the effectiveness of economic, social and political because the spiritual controls the physical. What is upholding a building is its foundation, the structure and that is where lasting reformation begins.

Foundational reformation begins from understanding of what is wrong spiritually and the solution or actions for implementation and restoration faster and better. For instance, the automobiles, electronic phones, and computers are better, faster with higher capacities now than before because of higher understanding and obedience to instruction or its usage application by man. Now there is a better spiritual system and understanding that must be obeyed for faster and better restoration, recovery and fulfillment in our lives, country and all over the world. This is a great choice and responsibility.

Individual Restructuring

This system of time and economic intelligence is a system of personal transformation and diverse knowledge. There can be no effective national transformation, development or recovery without personal and individual spiritual transformation of those that make up a country, region, community or a family. Don't be deceived when you see some people 'prospering' who don't know much or obey the higher spiritual powers. They may have only been reaping the works of a careless-carefree person. But in any case, they always end badly very quickly and they become examples of the worst case scenario. That is why the end will always justify the means. For you, it is better you do what you know, operate it by yourself, value it to create your own reward and you will have more satisfaction.

The reason that what you did or the works of your hand did not bring more advantages or success to you is because you failed to understand and operate time intelligence spiritually and that is what this model book is set to teach you. Receive it and operate it and see your greater success and advantages wherever you may be.

The Solution to Money

In the 21st Century economic recession, money, currencies reduced, depleted, diminished and was drained up globally and many wonder how and why. The irony is not that the there is no 'less value for money' and 'no too much money chasing fewer goods' as many economist would say but there is 'wrong value for money- it is called 'money-faithlessness' or 'money failure'. That is why the banks are struggling as well, they don't know where the monies are and it seems as if people are keeping more at home instead of banking them. Some blame it on technology improvement. But new solutions in technology should not kill banks but improve them but you can see it has failed in that regard. Therefore technology improvement is not the solution right now to money creation, multiplication and sustainability. Money seems to be nowhere to be found. I have heard and attached money importance to time. Some say time is money and that is true. Therefore if Time is corrosive, rust (which is the real problem of the world right now) then Money is corrosive, depleted as well. The Solution is that if Time is redeemed, then money can be refill again and fail not.

Time and Money

Money is time and wealth is created by time. Therefore, you authority and dominion of time create and establish your wealth in many areas directly and indirectly. Those mean that if you can manage time, you can manage money and the money you have or hold will not diminish as the case with others but used to create multiple benefits for you.

How is time money and wealth? The scripture the wisdom of God, the authority of God says *"If they obey and serve [him], they shall spend their days in prosperity, and their years in pleasures"*.(KJV) **Job 36:11**

The words 'days' or 'years' means time and it therefore means that a person's **prosperity is determine by 'daily'** by the operation of time

You must notice that they are two conditions attached in the above scripture: **Job 36:11**

1. That if we will obey this instructions <u>(of time and economic intelligence)</u>,
2. And if we serve (God, The Earth and Mankind)

With the above fulfilled, then we can turn our <u>days to prosperity</u> that is pleasurable or extending to many years (generations). Before we extend deeply into the two continuous which are the main tenets of this model book, let us briefly examine them as a process of God's mercy on us through the previous verses: Job 36: 5- 10. The summary is that we were actually using the wrong or ineffective idea to manage or money and prosperity until we apply the knowledge of time intelligence; therefore it is written:

Job 36: 5-7: *Behold, God [is] mighty, and despiseth not [any: he is] mighty in strength [and] wisdom.* *He preserveth not the life of the wicked: but giveth right to the poor.* *He withdraweth not his eyes from the righteous: but with kings [are they] on the throne; yea, he doth establish them for ever, and they are exalted.*	God is always merciful.
Job 36:8-10: *And if [they be] bound in fetters, [and] be holden in cords of affliction;* *Then he sheweth them their work, and their transgressions that they have exceeded.* *He openeth also their ear to discipline, and commandeth that they return from iniquity.*	The mercy of God is to teach us (open our eyes to) what we did wrong and what to do for our best result/reward

Therefore, the mercy of God to us now is teaching us Time and Economic intelligence as a way out of making our day prosperous as a service. A service is a business and a solution which should be paid for. We must serve first and then our pay is sure as it is written *"For God [is] not unrighteous to forget your work and labour of love, which ye have shewed toward his name, in that ye have ministered (served) to the saints, and do minister (serve)"* **Hebrews 6:10.** Now, The only way to serve (God, man and the earth) and to turn our days into prosperity is through Time Deoxidization because time became corrosive. It is a more personal service and action from your bedroom to order your prosperity because you MUST NOT allow time to remain corrosive against you.

PART THREE

UNDERSTANDING YOUR ACTION

Time Deoxidization

Time must be **deoxidized**, **neutralized** and **diffused** from its corrosive state now. In the spiritual it is called ***Time Redemption*** or ***Redeeming the TIME***. The challenge is that only a particular set of people in a **Global Union** can do it. And they must first be Christians; believers in Christ Jesus. Now every Christian not operating the Time Deoxidization process as a service law or commandment is in a state of foolishness as the unwise as it is written: *"Wherefore he saith, Awake thou that sleepest, and arise from the dead, and Christ shall give thee light. See then that ye walk circumspectly, **not as fools**, but as wise**, Redeeming the time**, because the days (times) are evil. Wherefore be **ye not unwise**, but understanding what the will of the Lord [is]"*. **Ephesians 5:14-17.** This is action time and it is better late than never if we must survive this worldwide onslaught.

There are (3) three Major Things about Time Deoxidization process. These include:-

1. Anything bad can happen to anyone who does not understand and operate Time Deoxidization process
2. <u>Non-Global</u> corporation, understanding and operation of <u>The Time deoxidization system</u> has been less effective and beneficial to anyone and the world.
3. The Global Partnership for the operation of time is the direct solution for Personal challenges, creativity/innovation and global solution to general and generational challenges.

The Time Deoxidization process or operation is a spiritual ordinance of dominion and leadership in global partnership. Time Deoxidization process is a great form of personal training advantage to <u>determine and secure</u> your wealth for you greatness and expression of God's love and goodness.

Take a Great Part in Your Destiny

No one is born to do a particular thing, read a particular course, marry a particular person but the <u>availability and personal training</u> determines them all and even more effectively with eternal benefit(s) by the help of God. Be available!

Expressing Faith and Believe

A man asked what could be the thin line (difference) between faith and believe, and he was told that; to have faith is <u>to hear</u> something or an instruction, and to believe is to act based on what you heard or receive by following the instructions. The scripture says "<u>faith comes by hearing</u>"- (Romans 10:17) and that we <u>speak</u> (act) because we <u>believe (2Cor 4:13)</u>. This why James instructed that we should show our faith by our works (actions) as it is written: *"Yes, a man may say, Thou hast faith, and I have works: shew me thy faith without thy works, <u>and I will shew thee my faith by my works</u>"* *"Was not Abraham our father justified by works, when he had <u>offered Isaac</u> his son upon the altar? Seest thou how faith wrought with his works, and by works was faith made perfect?"* **James 2:18, 21-22**

Believe your faith- and faith your believe

1. **Believe Your faith-** When you believe your faith. You primary act- put what you hear to test in order to order your experience or receive the promise that that is attached to your faith. In order words, there is no effectiveness of any instruction you receive, unless you act on it.

2. **Faith Your Believe:** When you faith your believe, you speak it out, you teach it to others, you instruct others based on it and you also tell others who care to listen the result of what you acted upon. This is to the intent that God be glorified and that many would have faith and believe in Him also.

All the above may be to the glory of God but intensively for our creative favour and benefits. Where is your believe from your faith? Go ahead and apply the understanding and obey the instruction of this Spiritual System in a One

Global Partnership. God exists and succeeds in partnership (Father, Son and the Holy Spirit) as with man and nature. Therefore if you must help and succeed globally starting from where you are, then you must be in an effective partnership globally. We can create a beautiful difference.

It is your faith and believe (that set you free); that what is called truth (experience, knowledge or action) according to divine instruction. Therefore He said *"...Daughter, be of good comfort; <u>thy faith hath made thee whole</u>. And the woman was made whole from that hour"*. **Matthew 9:22** for *"you shall know the truth, and the truth shall make you free."* **John 8:32**

There is a Partnership- HSPS

Every creation is through an effective partnership of people and things. God expresses such partnership as God the Father, Son and The Holy Ghost. The mystery that must be understood here is that of effective partnership to save the earth and for us to create money and wealth effectively. Money and wealth is in every land (the earth and the world). Our challenge is how to create it effectively and one of such means is through our effectively partnership as people with one understanding and effective commitment of time, energy and finance in any particular location that we may be. Time deoxidization is the key and we must do this in an effective global partnership for a global result because of our global nature. Such partnership now exist worldwide as HSPS. HSPS means Homeland Security and Prosperity System. HSPS is the ONLY worldwide partnership of the Christian race and a Network System of good people; organizations and governments to effective deoxidize time and to create and establish our wealth. HSPS has both natural and supernatural benefits. God gave us instruction that HSPS must be advanced and operated daily in every city or nation to deliver us and many from all forms of challenges and evil including natural disasters, terrorism and bio war (virus and disease spread), economic challenges and global warming and to turn them to Christ. HSPS teaches and advocates worldwide for personal security and prosperity, Peace Advocacy, Conflict Resolution, Knowledge Advancement, Job Creation, Entrepreneurship, Business Development and Financing, Law Enforcement, Climate Change Management etc. _Right now, nothing (business, government, organization etc) is working as they should in the world except through us by the service of time deoxidization in partnership_ which we are operating and hereby recommend.

THE TWO LEGS OF HSPS

HSPS has a business/Entrepreneurship Model with a Spiritual Intelligence Effectiveness. This is analyzed below:-

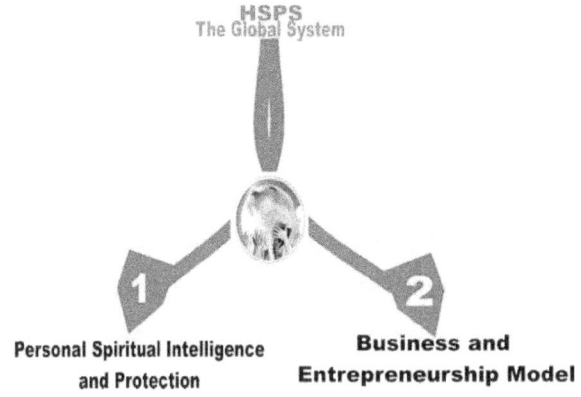

1. **HSPS Spiritual Intelligence Effectiveness** provides access to:
a. Divine Time Management
b. Overcoming Temptation/Personal Challenges
c. High Spiritual Protection System

2. HSPS Business /Entrepreneurship Model provides access to
a. Business Development
b. Financial and Start-up Capital
c. Global Fund
d. Global Civil Service System

With over one billion people joining HSPS worldwide, you stand a chance of contributing and creating your own financial success as much as you want. This is because for everyone that you help with HSPS membership and Operation to, you get $12 or ₦3000 only for your own personal and business use and it is transferable to your loved ones. Any financial success system without a spiritual protection is a waste of time and energy and resources. HSPS worldwide partnership and membership operation grants a person divine protection through universal life energy synchronization. With this a person can determine how and when to die. *The reason for the financial obligation of HSPS is for effective partnership and for us to be able to create* _finance from the available money worldwide or in our location for godly uses._

HSPS- Homeland Security and Prosperity System is a support System of Prayers and global peace advocacy and intersession. **It must be used by**

a. Every Minister of the Gospel worldwide irrespective of Church inclination.
b. Everyone who desires to know and understand God better.
c. Everyone who desires peace personally and otherwise.
d. Every Church of Christ in the world
e. Every child of God worldwide.

It can also be advanced or operated also by

a. Families for the loved one's success and protection.
b. Business men and corporate bodies for increased business profit and breakthrough
c. Social-political organization and groups for their own success

d. Youths to raise start-up business and personal development capital

Your Personal Exposition Guide

You have only been told that there is a Time De-oxidization process to creating and establish money and security, but not the definite time and what to do at such time. And you need to become a Global Partner in such system by your definite financial commitment, and then your time and energy synchronization becomes effective. This is how your <u>Personal Exposition Guide</u> containing those Secret can be printed (on Demand) and mailed or emailed to you.

What is your Finance Used For?

You will need to sacrifice N5000 or $18 for your partnership and Exposition Guide. 40% (N2000 or $6) of what you pay as a onetime Global Partnership fee is used to print your HSPS Exposition Guide and mailed to you wherever you may be worldwide and 60% of which is given to another HSPS Global Partner who introduces HSPS to you. You or any other Partner receives 60% (N3000 or $12USD) each time parallel and continuously for life with every new registration of someone worldwide. Although this reward is optional but it is with the intension that the children of God help each other to create their own personal and business finance for their use in goodness and in faith. *This is our divine time and economic Intelligence (National Economic Policy) to mop up the available resources and to multiply same in business and welfare*. It is godly approach.

The TIME IS NOW

You need to know what to do now. Those who appreciate knowledge appreciate everything.

Register, Make your Global Contribution and Receive Your Exposition/Operation Guide. You can also attend our global discussion group offline and offline. Use the Website www.hspsworldwide.com

Understanding Your Power with God

Power is a network, an order, an organizational process of people and time. Therefore, the scripture reads: *"Let every soul be subject unto the higher powers. For there is <u>no power</u> but of God: <u>the powers that be are ordained of God</u>. Whosoever therefore <u>resisteth the power,</u> resisteth the <u>ordinance of God</u>: and they that resist shall receive to themselves damnation"*. **Romans 13:1-2.** The wisdom of God is the power of God; as a result, the wisdom of God is acquired or accessed by the ordinance of God for our profiting as it is written: *"But we speak the <u>wisdom of God</u> in a mystery, [even] the hidden [wisdom], <u>which God ordained</u> before the world unto our glory"* **1 Corinthians 2:7.** It is my hope that you do not reject this ordinance of God now. Whoever disobeys and rejects this time ordinance rejects the power of God.

The Power to Make Wealth

It is God by ordinance that gives us power to make or create wealth as it is written *"But thou shalt remember the LORD thy God: for [it is] he that giveth thee power to get wealth, that he may establish his covenant which he sware unto thy fathers, as [it is] this day".* **Deuteronomy 8:18.** Time De-oxidization is the power of God to make wealth right now and this is how it will be in the world to come, and that is how it has been, except we did not know or failed to comply. Is it not written that *"The thing that hath been, it [is that] which shall be; and that which is done [is] that which shall be done: and [there is] no new [thing] under the sun. Is there [any] thing whereof it may be said, See, this [is] new? it hath been already of old time, which was before us.* **Ecclesiastes 1:9-10**

Wake up and stand out now. It is time

"I know the devil; the devil in me is my ignorance"

Time Remains Evil Until Redeemed

Time is a divine structure or designed as evil unless it is redeemed. It must be redeemed by us in order that we should create our reward and partake in determining and enforcing our success or destiny. This applies to everyone irrespective of location or colour. God is a design as well Time. God has designed time for good or evil permission by a man in his life. The natural state, time remains evil as it is written *"Sufficient for the day [is] the evil of it"* **Matthew 6:34**. Day is time and full of evil. And that is why is written *"See then that ye walk circumspectly, not as fools, but as wise, Redeeming the time, because the days are evil"* **Ephesians 5:15-16**. Consequently, time is a design such that if you don't redeem it, evil occurrences are permitted in your life to which you cannot control them. And this is primarily because you lost control of the right TIME in the first place.

The Natural VS the Supernatural

A person should understand his/her natural and supernatural standing to order personal success and this is how ideal or principled life can be. It is a supernatural design that everyone is always in danger of nature. This is not that God is wicked but provides us with opportunity to contribute to our success supernaturally and to understand Him.

It is natural that we look like our parents or relatives physically and/or in behavoiur. It is also natural that we behave within some identifiable traits of our environment or location. Again, it is natural that everyone has done something wrong and also some good. Personally, it is natural that, what you did wrong should affect you negatively and what you did well should affect you positively.

Therefore, it is natural that what your parents did positively should affect your positively and vice verse unless there are rejected or accepted by you. This is what some call generational curse or blessing. All things and everyone take a natural effect unless over ruled by the supernatural order. The supernatural is an order of higher and better power to overrule the excesses of nature and to establish its goodness. What the above structure mean is that everyone- who is of age must deliver himself from his own mistakes, the mistake of others (parents, family, friend and even the environment, city or country) and as well to establish the associated goodness or benefit. This is a simple process called life and must be done daily by everyone who desires to live decently, independently and successfully with the help of God. This is how we must deliver our selves daily and others inclusive as Paul would instruct Timothy saying: *"Watch your life and doctrine closely. Persevere in them, because if you do, you will save both yourself and your hearers (listens to your instructions) (NIV)* **1 Timothy 4:16.**

We know that we have been saved by the works of Christ and beveling in Him. But this only gives us a better understanding (of what to do) and to have better results as it is written *"God… Who hath saved us, and called us with an holy calling, not according to our works, but according to his own purpose and grace, which was given us in Christ Jesus before the world began"* **2Timothy 1:9**

How to Overrule the Natural

The process of life is in a routine. A routine is a regulation, a regular activity to achieve a purpose. A routine may involve the commitment of time, energy and financial resources. A routine can be called a religion. Religion is a process of reaching God by one or two persons at the same time.

The Time Ordinance is the real process of life (a routine and religion) by which a person can overrule the natural with the supernatural, defend his/herself, understand God and protect others.

Keeping the time ordinance is <u>the most foolish thing to do on earth</u> *"Because the foolishness of God is wiser than men; and the weakness of God is stronger than men"* **1 Corinthians 1:25**. It is like subjecting you to a prayer time or religion.

But a person must be under authority to exercise authority. In all remember that

For example, the President came under the authority of the Election body (complied with its procedures/arrangements) as well as received the authority of the voters to become a president and to exercise presidential authority.

Therefore, do all you can to be subjected to the Time Ordinance so that you make all other powers of the enemy subject to you. And this is how we can make personal success in all areas of our lives. It doesn't matter who you lack or needs now; taking the operation of the Time Ordinance is the greatest key of this age to make progress.

In conclusion, the time ordinance is the best way 'to be the best you can be' because you have control over the natural and to enforce the supernatural upon your life.

Apply an Action

Contact the nearest Consultant who told you about HSPS or Register at the website www.hspsworldwide.com and use them as your sponsor. Every value must have a cost. Every effective partnership involves TIME, ENERGY and FINANCIAL commitment or sacrifice. *"Now every Christian not operating the Time Deoxidization process as a service law or commandment is in a state of foolishness as the unwise"* Make a choice to help and to succeed now. Your Registration and financial commitment completes your partnership and gives you access to the TIME Intelligence by which you must operate and what you must say at such specific time. It is very difficult to find a System that works for everyone according to their various needs, but we are happy to let you know that Time Deoxidization does so and much more as End Time revelation of God. It is a solution to heal the whole world. Time De-

Oxidization is a great privilege to us, by us and through us.

Every creation and effective multiplication is done in a partnership order.

Join the Only Global Partnership for effective Time Deoxidization.

Mr. Noah preached for 120 years and yet many perished by the flood. It doesn't matter if others agree to Time De-Oxidation with you or not. But practice it and create your own reward like Noah and his family.

www.hspsworldwide.com

You GOT IT!

Respect and Honour The Difference

We must respect difference in corporation and success definition if we must succeed and establish progress. With the difference in time, people, knowledge and understanding, rewards are created in diverse forms.

The Difference may call for a holy fight for success. This is because, where there is no fight, there is no victor. Life is a fight and a day is a fight.

<u>Today</u> You are fighting against you inabilities <u>yesterday</u> for a better <u>tomorrow.</u> There is a way to fight to lose and a way to fight to win or to lose. A fight is not won by strength but by strategies.

HSPS is The Difference

The Global Partnership through HSPS is the beautiful difference we need to launch the world into a new realm of freedom and it must begin with us. It is the best way to fight, serve and win.

Money where are you? Where is money?

Gone are the days when people get FREE monies or steal money easily in Nigeria and round about the world. The Government is looking for money- (some say half salaries/wages), or implement projects the banks are looking for the money- they are now retrenching their staff and sending people to rake in the available monies from the hand of petty traders and others who are also complaining of not having the money. This is a worldwide affair. Therefore, we need a worldwide solution and it must begin with you.

The Beginning and the End

Find out how to define the end of a thing from its beginning. Until a thing has a planned end from its beginning, it is not supposed to be fulfilled.

Life is a fight and service and a day is a fight.

There is a way to fight/serve to lose and a way to fight/serve to win or to lose. A fight is not only won by strength but largely by strategies.

Find out in this Model book: **Time and Economic Intelligence** for the Best way to Fight, Serve and Win.

www.hspswordwide.come

knowing more and doing more now

www.ingramcontent.com/pod-product-compliance
Lightning Source LLC
Chambersburg PA
CBHW070403190526
45169CB00003B/1093